# Music for Clarinet & Piano

## ADVANCED LEVEL
## Volume 2

To access audio visit:
**www.halleonard.com/mylibrary**

Enter Code
7701-1904-1530-7370

ISBN 978-1-59615-253-3

## Music Minus One

EXCLUSIVELY DISTRIBUTED BY

## HAL•LEONARD®

Visit Hal Leonard Online at
**www.halleonard.com**

Contact Us:
**Hal Leonard**
7777 West Bluemound Road
Milwaukee, WI 53213
Email: info@halleonard.com

In Europe contact:
**Hal Leonard Europe Limited**
42 Wigmore Street
Marylebone, London, W1U 2RN
Email: info@halleonardeurope.com

In Australia contact:
**Hal Leonard Australia Pty. Ltd.**
4 Lentara Court
Cheltenham, Victoria, 3192 Australia
Email: info@halleonard.com.au

CONTENTS

# PERFORMANCE GUIDE
## COMMENTARY BY HAROLD WRIGHT

### RABAUD
#### Solo de Concours

This is one of the famous contest pieces of the Paris Conservatory. It is musically uncomplicated, and needs an imaginative approach. In the florid beginning, it will be helpful to group note patterns together, and use certain notes as anchor points. This will help you to gain control of the long passages, and the scales will not sound like dry exercises.

The Largo is a little reminiscent of Bach. The long, sustained lines have many musical possibilities. Keep them flowing; if this section is allowed to sag, it will be very dull!

The Allegro will sound best if you play it with a feeling of one beat to the bar. Give a special stress to the top of the phrase. When you reach the 6/8 section, continue the feeling of one beat to the bar. The tempo should remain constant, whether you are playing in 2/4 or 6/8 time. The composer has given us a feeling of accelerando in those instances where the triplet figures change to groups of sixteenth notes; it will not be necessary to play faster, since the accelerandos are "built-in!"

### MOZART
#### Concerto, K. 622
#### 1st Movement: Allegro moderato

This Concerto is a difficult piece to play well. The rhythmic figures must be played evenly; a sloppy rubato would destroy the clarity so necessary to the classical style. You will need to create a variety of mood in this music. Don't play too fast; you need time to expand and express your musical ideas.

Whenever musically possible, the trills should begin on the upper note. They should be played evenly. Musical content will very often suggest the most effective articulation. For example, this descending phrase should be played quickly and in a declamatory manner:

There are many opportunities for smooth, lyric playing. Study the following section:

You will need to know the accompaniment as well as the solo part. Many times the ornamental solo lines are accompaniment figures. The piano has the musical interest in the following section:

This movement ends with a series of brilliant arpeggios, trill-like figures outlining the tonic chord, a chromatic scale, and a long, dramatic shake. Mozart has provided a full bag of tricks for an ambitious clarinetist!

Harold Wright

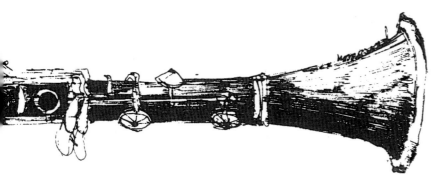

# SOLO DE CONCOURS

HENRI RABAUD
Arr. by Paul Dahm

(5' 30")

17 seconds to measure 5

17 seconds to measure 9

6

8

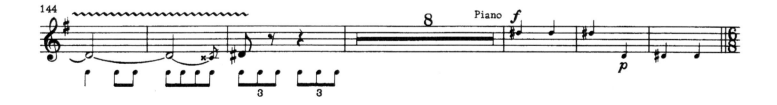

# CONCERTO, K. 622

WOLFGANG A. MOZART
Revised by Jean Albert
de la Tournerie

33 Solo

p dolce, senza cresc.

38

espress.

poco

p

p

43

p

f

46

p

espress.

f

50

senza dim.

tr

2

p dolce

56

f sostenuto 3

3

3

3

60 espress.

sempre f

dolce

63

cresc.

f

68

f espress.

3

f

p

110 Solo
*p*

112
*cresc.*

114
*f*                                    *sempre f*

117
*f*

119
*f*

122
*cresc.*                        *f*  *mf*        *cresc.*

125

127
*poco*        3   3   3

Piano
131

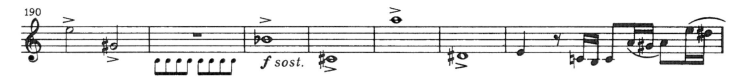

254 Solo

259

262 Piano

Solo

267

271

274

277

281

285

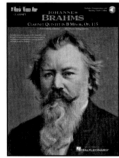

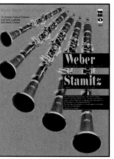